– 10th Anniversary Edition –

Ten years ago when we began the discovery process of writing this book our working title was "Louise Goes to School". We had spent a day traveling to different villages looking for a girl who would be our model. When we found Louise, she just loved to be in front of the camera having her picture taken. She was a natural. It was not until after the book was written and the photographs taken that we started the process of picking a cover photo. We chose the cover photograph for the bright colors of the fisherman's boat. It was then that we noticed the fisherman had named his boat in Creole "La vi ti moun", which translates "Life of a Child". It was a goose bumps moment and we knew that we needed to change the title from "Louise Goes to School" to "Life of a Child".

LA VI TI MOUN

Life of a Child

A Story of Child Sponsorship in Haiti

La vi Ti Moun: Life of a Child
"La vi Ti Moun: Life of a Child," copyright ©1998 New Missions

Editor, creative concepts: Kim Jackson
Graphic Design: Antoinette Tesoriero Griffin

Published by Presidents Publishing
P.O. Box 2727, Orlando, Florida 32802

Library of Congress Control Number: 2009905121

Lécole New Missions
3644 Louise Nada Charles
ID Issued: Feb-98
Enrolled: 12/13/91
Birthdate: 11/01/87
Sex: girl
Program: LAS-04
Village: LaSalle, Haiti

Glossary

Creole	Pronunciation	English
lavi ti moun	(lahvee tee moon)	life of a child
Port-au-Prince	(Paw-tah-Prens)	the capital city of Haiti
tonton	(TOHN tohn)	uncle
banann	(bah nahn)	cooking bananas
gourdes	(goo-ds)	Haitian money
ti gason	(tee gah sohn)	young boy
Creole	(Cray-ol)	the common language of Haiti
blan moun	(blahn moon)	white people
mwe regret sa	(mweh raygret sah)	I'm sorry
li bel	(lee bell)	it is beautiful
lavi Kris la	(lah vee Krees la)	the life of Christ

Louise loves to walk along the beach by the sea.

She stops to watch the boats sail by. There are fishing boats, huge container ships, and small cargo boats. The cargo boats carry sugar cane and charcoal from the villages to the big market in Port-au-Prince.

Louise often stops to talk with Tonton Jean. He sits on a boat waiting to sort the catch the fishermen bring ashore. While he waits, Tonton Jean tells stories about Haiti long ago–stories of pirates and buried treasures, French princesses and beautiful plantations, slaves and cruel masters.

Louise remembers the stories when she goes to her special place under the mango tree. As the sunlight drifts through the leaves, she imagines she is digging up treasure left by pirates.

Sometimes Louise pretends to write down Tonton Jean's stories so she can have them forever. She uses a stick to clear a patch of ground and then tries to think of the shapes of the letters she has seen on the magazine pages that cover the walls of her hut.

"Louise, Louise, come here!" She hears her mother's voice in the distance. Louise looks at the sun setting behind the coconut palm trees. It is time for her to gather sticks for the fire so her mother can cook dinner.

The fire is soon hot enough for cooking. Louise squats beside her mother and looks into the pot. Today is not a good day: only banann. Louise knows their banann must last a long time, so her mother has cooked only two.

But no matter how careful they are, the banann will soon be gone and her mother will have to beg the fishermen to give her a few fish. If they have caught enough, they will let her take fish to another village to sell. Her mother will have to pay back the fishermen, but if she sells all the fish she will have money to buy rice. What a treat that would be!

The next morning, well before the chickens begin scratching in the yard, Louise wakes up. Her little brother, Pierre, is crying loudly. Not even sucking on sugar cane will quiet him. Long after the sun has made the colors of the day–the green leaves and the blue sky–Pierre keeps crying.

"Is Pierre going to be all right?" Louise asks.

Her mother touches Pierre's forehead.

"He is very hot. I know they could help him at the medical clinic in Bord Mer, but..."

"What, mother?"

"I did not sell fish yesterday. I have no gourdes."

Louise looks at her mother's worried face. "Let's go anyway," she says. "Maybe they will still help us."

Louise's mother puts on her blue-and-white dress and wraps Pierre in a bath towel. Louise feels very grown-up carrying her mother's bag as they begin walking to Bord Mer. The long walk finally rocks Pierre to sleep.

They are grateful to see the stone wall leading to the clinic. The gate squeaks behind them, and they join the others waiting to see the doctor. Louise looks around. There are so many unfamiliar faces. She sits very still beside her mother. One by one the people disappear into the clinic. At last it is Pierre's turn.

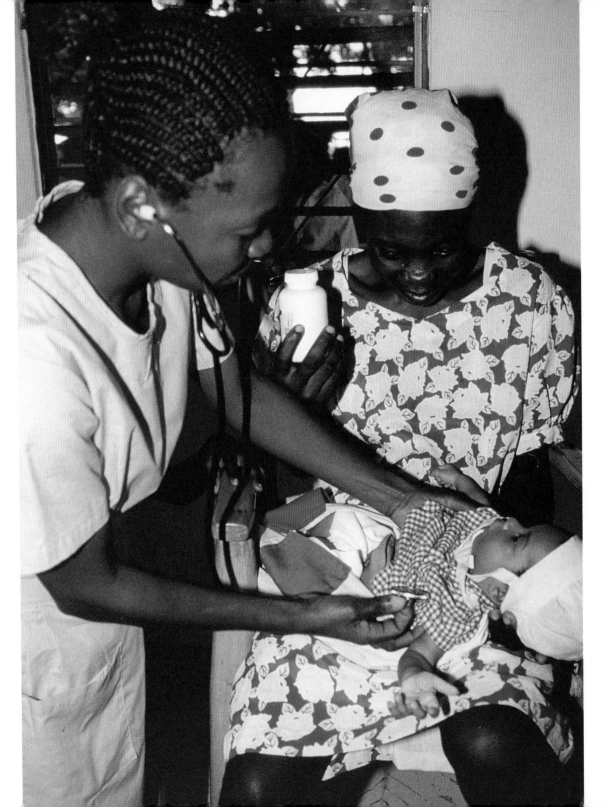

The doctor listens to Pierre's chest and takes his temperature. Then she looks in his ears. "Ah ha," she says. "That is the problem. I think your ti gason has an ear infection. I will have the pharmacist prepare medicine to make him well. Pierre is nearly asleep now. Leave him here for a while. When you come back I will tell you what to do."

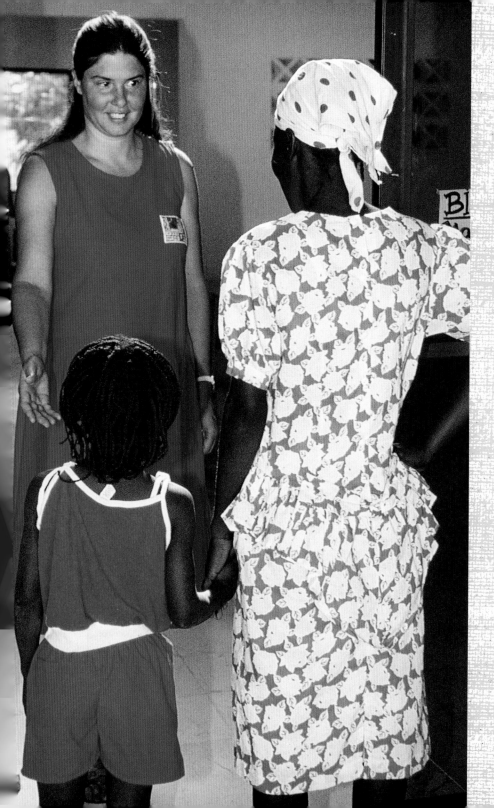

As Louise and her mother are walking out the door, they meet a woman in a red dress. "What is your name?" the woman asks Louise in Creole.

Louise is not used to talking with blan moun. She hides her face.

"What is your name?" the woman asks again.

Louise still does not answer.

"She is Louise," her mother says.

"Where do you come from?" the woman asks.

"La Salle, Miss."

"Oh. Does Louise go to school there?"

"Mwe regret sa," Louise's mother replies. "We have just moved here from Jacmel to be near my brother. My husband is gone . . . There is no money for school . . ." Her voice trails off as she turns to leave.

"No, wait," says the lady in the red dress.

"My name is Miss Julie. Please come with me. I have something to show you."

Louise and her mother follow Miss Julie into another building. She invites them to sit down at a table. Then she opens a big book. It has plastic on the pages, and underneath there are photographs of people. Louise looks at them. Some of the ladies are wearing pretty dresses. Other people are holding animals that do not look like the pigs and goats in her village. One family is standing in front of a tree that has shiny things hanging on it.

What does all this mean? Louise wonders, but she is too shy to ask. Miss Julie seems to know what she is thinking.

"These are photographs of people in other countries. Many of them live in the United States or Canada. They give money each month so children like you can go to school and come to the clinic. These people are called sponsors. If you would like," Miss Julie says, looking at Louise's mother, "we could find a sponsor for Louise and then she could go to school."

Louise stares at the photographs again, trying to understand what Miss Julie is saying. *Are there really people in other countries who would help me go to school? Can it be true? And even if it is, will my mother let me go?*

Louise listens to every word Miss Julie says. She tells them to come back tomorrow to have Louise's photograph taken and to be measured for a school uniform.

Louise follows her mother out the door in a daze. She came with her sick baby brother, and she is leaving with the promise of school!

The doctor is waiting for them back at the clinic. Pierre's medicine is ready. Louise's mother listens carefully to the instructions. Pierre is to drink two capfuls, three times each day. The nurse asks Louise's mother if she can read the label on the medicine bottle. When she shakes her head "no," the nurse explains the directions three times to be sure she will remember.

Louise listens, too. *One day*, she says to herself, *One day I will be able to read the words on the bottle. All of them.*

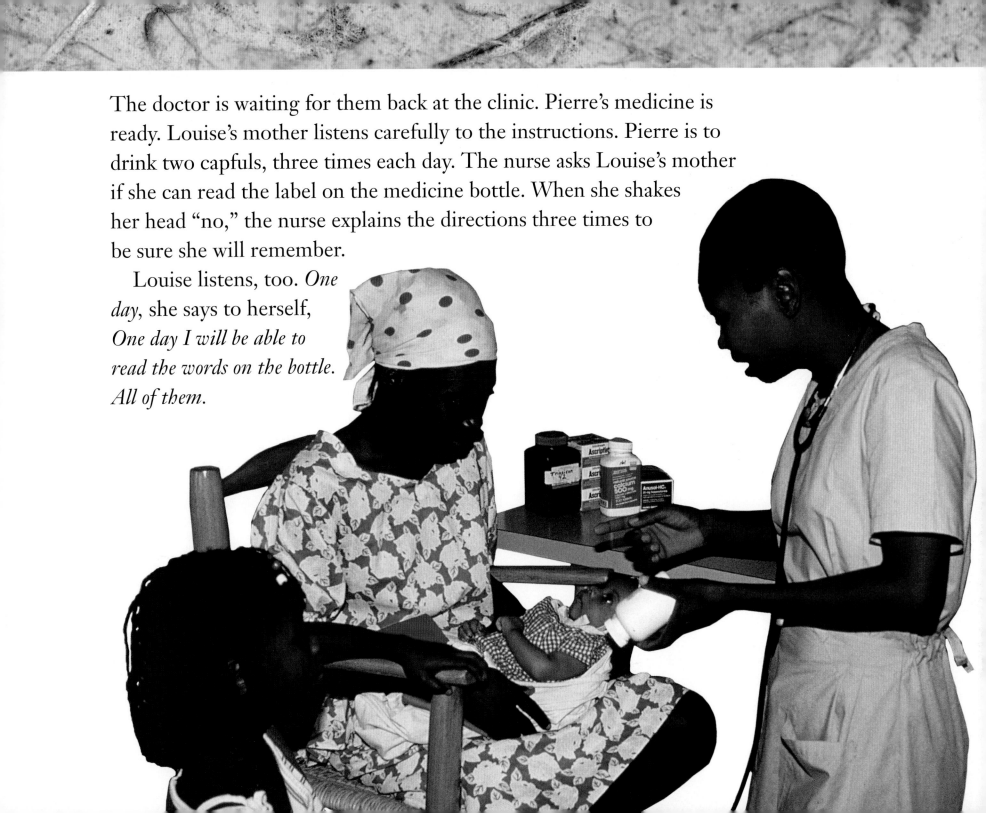

That night Louise can barely sleep. She closes her eyes, but her excitement keeps her awake. When the chickens start scratching the dirt in the yard, she jumps from her bed. Pierre stays with Tonton Jean, and Louise and her mother set out for Bord Mer once again.

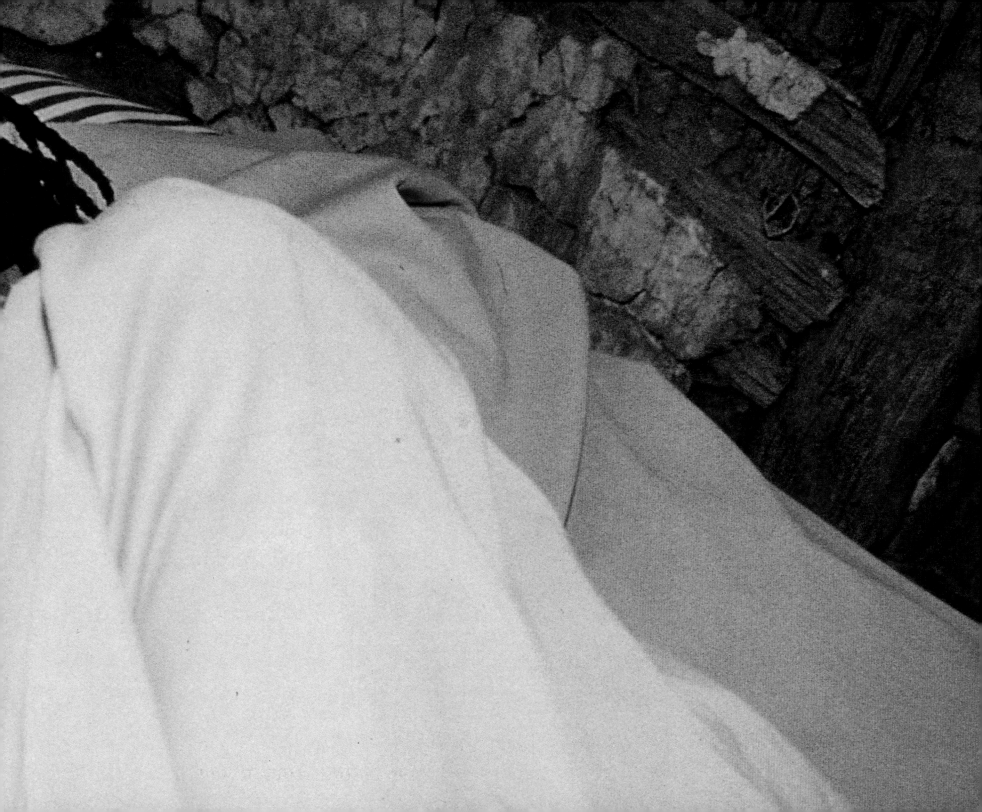

Miss Julie is waiting for them. First Louise has her photograph taken. She has never seen a camera before. She thinks, *Why should I smile just because someone asks me to?* but she tries her best.

Next Miss Julie takes her to a small room with shelves piled high with folded fabric. Louise loves the yellow-and-white checks. Miss Julie measures to see how tall Louise is, and then gives her a piece of fabric.

Now it is time to find the seamstress who makes the school uniforms. Louise watches in awe as she cuts the fabric and lays it on the sewing machine. Louise likes the sound of the needle and thread poking through the fabric again and again. *Swish-swash*, *swish-swash*. Louise can hardly wait for the seamstress to finish the uniform.

Finally it is time to try it on. Miss Julie gives
Louise a mirror so she can look at herself in her new dress.

"Li bel, li bel," Louise whispers to herself.

Now Louise cannot stop smiling. She feels like the
princess in one of Tonton Jean's stories.

When they return to the office, a man calls Louise to his desk. "Here is your school identification card, Louise. It is on a red cord so you will not lose it. Bring it with you to school every day. It tells the teacher many things she needs to know. See, I have punched a hole in it to show that you have a new uniform. Tomorrow you will wear the card to school and show it to the teacher. I will tell her to expect you," he tells Louise.

The next morning Louise chews on sugar cane for breakfast. It doesn't fill her stomach, but today she doesn't care. Today is school day!

Her mother braids Louise's hair in a special way, and she puts on her brand-new uniform. When Louise sees other children from the village walking past her hut on their way to school, she calls out, "Wait for me! I am a school girl, too!"

At school she goes to class with the other children. *Is it the right one?* Louise holds her breath as the teacher reads her card. "Welcome to our class," she says in a gentle voice.

"I am Miss Manite. You may sit here," she says, pointing to a nearby bench.

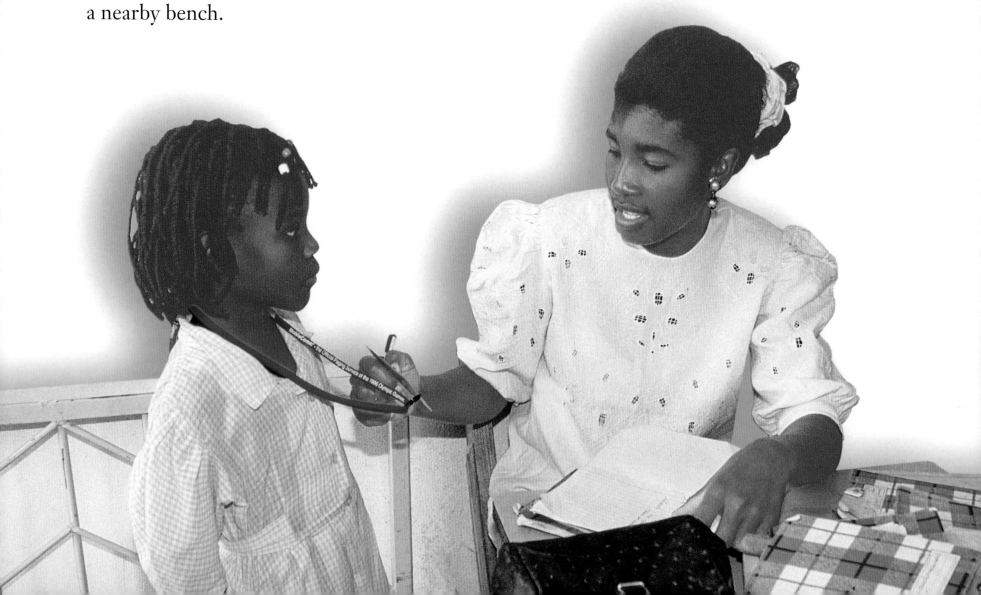

Miss Manite starts to write on the blackboard. When the other students are working in their books, she calls Louise to the front of the classroom and begins teaching her the alphabet. Time goes by very quickly. Soon the lunch bell rings.

Louise follows her class to the pavilion. On the way they pass the kitchen where their meal is prepared. The smell is so good it makes Louise's stomach rumble.

Louise gets in line behind some older boys. She watches them and follows what they do. A woman hands her a bowl piled high with rice and beans.

Louise finds a place to sit
and begins to eat. The food
is more delicious than she
had imagined. When she
is finished, she thinks, *So
this is how it feels to have a
full stomach.*

Louise joins the other students who are waiting for the bell to ring, calling them to afternoon classes. They wander past the vendors who sit behind the fence selling crackers and candy. Louise has no money, but it doesn't matter. For once she is not hungry, and seeing other people eating doesn't make her feel sad today.

When school is over for the week, Louise's mother tells her, "Now every Saturday you will go draw water from the village well. Then I will wash your pretty school uniform for you."

Louise loves to stand on her tiptoes to hang the wet clothes high on the cactus hedge. She knows the clothes will dry before the sun goes down.

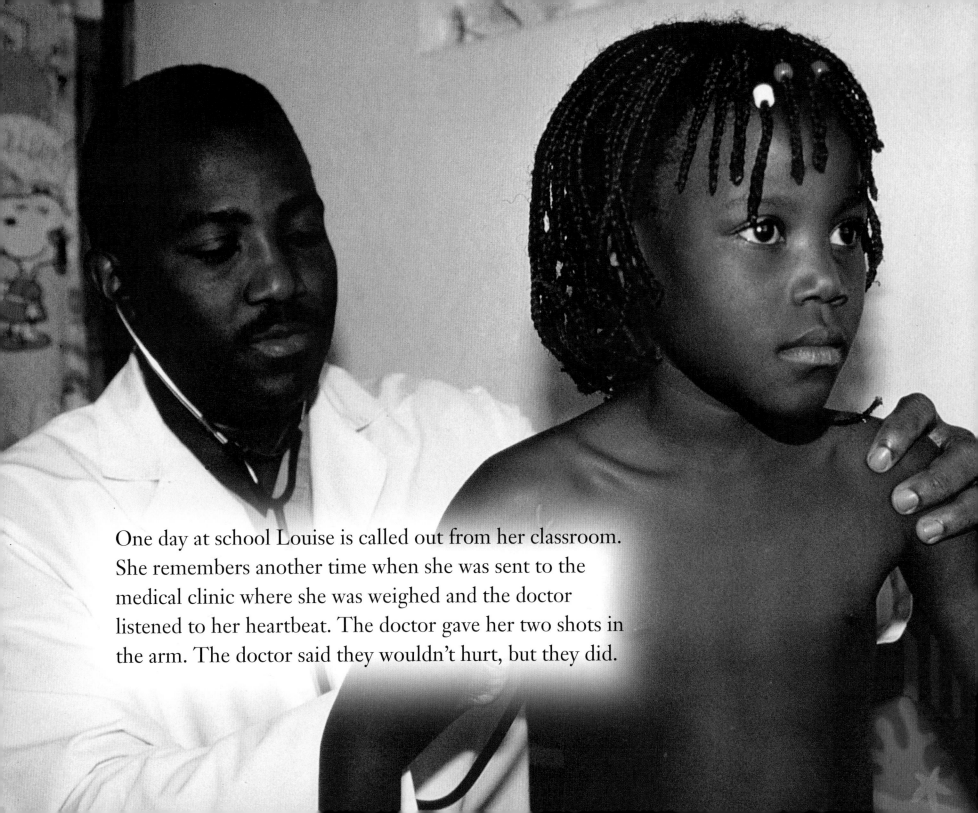

One day at school Louise is called out from her classroom. She remembers another time when she was sent to the medical clinic where she was weighed and the doctor listened to her heartbeat. The doctor gave her two shots in the arm. The doctor said they wouldn't hurt, but they did.

This time when Louise is called from class she is led to the office. Rene is smiling. "Here, I have something for you," he says, holding out a package. Louise remembers other students telling her that packages sometimes come from sponsors, but this seems too good to be true.

Has this package come all the way from the United States? she wonders. Her hands tremble as she opens it. Inside she finds crayons, scissors, stickers, and barrettes for her hair! There is even an envelope with money in it, and a letter from Mr. and Mrs. Geno saying that Rene is to help Louise buy a Bible storybook written in Creole.

Louise sits with her new treasures surrounding her. She is too happy to speak.

Rene says he will write a thank-you letter for her if she will tell him what to say. Now the words tumble out of Louise's mouth:

Good day. Thank you for what you have done for me. Today I received the very first present in my life. I love school and I go to church. I pray for God to bless you.

Then she colors her best picture for Mr. and Mrs. Geno, and writes her name at the bottom of the page, all by herself.

Soon Louise is writing more than her name. Now when she goes to her secret place under the mango tree she knows all the shapes and letters that form the words of Tonton Jean's stories. As she writes with her stick in the sand, she thinks about what Miss Manite told her on the last day of school before vacation: *You are a good student, Louise. I am proud of you!*

Louise is proud, too, but she didn't tell her teacher why. Only her Tonton Jean knows, because Louise still goes to the beach where he sits waiting for the fishermen. She listens to Tonton Jean's wonderful stories for a while, and then, very carefully, she reads a story to him.

About The Mission

To find out more about
sponsoring a child call us
or visit our website.

New Missions
P. O. Box 2727
Orlando, Fl 32802
800-937-4842
info@newmissions.org
www.newmissions.org

Illiteracy —not being able to read or write—is a form of blindness. To teach children to read and write is to give them sight and vision for their lives.

In many countries, getting an education is taken for granted. But that is not the case in Haiti, where illiteracy affects 70% of the population.

Louise goes to a New Missions' school in Haiti. Her "blindness," caused by illiteracy, is being cured. New worlds of opportunity will be within her reach. This is made possible only because someone made a commitment to sponsor Louise.

There are thousands of children like Louise who are in need of sponsorship. To find out more about sponsoring a child call us or visit our website.

Child sponsorship is made possible through New Missions, a nondenominational Christian organization founded by George DeTellis, Sr. and his wife, Jeanne. Working on the Leogane Plain since 1983, New Missions currently has 22 preschools, 22 elementary schools, a high school, and a college, with a total enrollment of over 9000 students.

New Missions also has 22 churches, and a medical clinic that cares for nearly 1000 Haitians each month.

Louise today is sponsored by George DeTellis. Louise is attending the New Missions high school in Haiti. She is still living in the village of La Salle with her family.

Haiti

———	International boundary
– · – · –	Department boundary
★	National capital
CAYES	Department capital
┼┼┼┼	Railroad
———	Surfaced road
– – – –	Unsurfaced road
✈	Airfield
⚓	Principal port
⚓	Secondary port

△ Spot elevations in meters

Scale 1:1,000,000

Populated places
Port-au-Prince - 1,100,000
● 25,000 and above
○ 5,000 to 25,000
• Under 5,000

Kilometers
0   10   20   30   40   50

Nautical Miles
0   10   20   30   40   50

Statute Miles
0   10   20   30   40   50

Lambert Conformal Conic Projection, standard parallels 17°20'N and 22°40'N

About Haiti

Haiti occupies the western third of the island of Hispaniola; the Dominican Republic makes up the rest of the island. Haiti is located 700 miles southeast of Florida.

- The capital is Port-au-Prince.

- The name *Haiti* means "mountainous."

- Haiti's landmass is approximately the size of the state of Maryland.

- Haiti's population is 9 million.

- Haiti ranks as the most "food-insecure" country in the Western Hemisphere, and the second most insecure in the world.

- The majority of the population does not have ready access to safe drinking water, adequate medical care, or sufficient food.

- A Haitian's life expectancy at birth is 57 years.

- The mortality rate for Haitian children under five years of age is 13 times greater than that for children in the United States.

- The Gross National Product per capita is estimated at $1400, although this figure disguises tremendous variations in income distribution. In fact, per capita income of more than 80% of the population is estimated at less than $150.

- Few social assistance programs exist, and the lack of employment opportunities remains one of the most critical problems facing the economy, along with soil erosion and political instability.

(Sources of statistics: USAID; 2008 State of the World's Children; UNICEF; The 2009 World Factbook; Haiti Consular Information Sheet)